Unbelievable Pictures and Facts About Golden Retrievers

By: Olivia Greenwood

Introduction

Golden retrievers have wonderful natures and extremely lovable dogs. They are great at being a best friend and a companion. They also make excellent therapy dogs. Today you will get the opportunity to learn all about this truly wonderful dogs.

Are golden retriever dogs very popular in America?

The answer is yes, golden retrievers are extremely popular dogs. They are loved and adored by people all over America.

Are golden retriever dogs very smart?

Golden retrievers are actually extremely clever dogs. In fact, they are one of the smartest dog breeds which exist to date.

Does the golden retriever dog breed enjoy swimming?

These dogs love swimming so much. They really do love to be around water and every time they are near water they will try to swim.

Are there any additional reasons to use golden retrievers?

Yes, many people make use of golden retriever for therapy dogs. They make fantastic therapy dogs. They have been known to be real heroes and helpers to people who have needed them the most.

What do these dogs do for the government?

Golden retrievers often work for the government as sniffer dogs. They have an excellent sense of smell. They also have a tendency to work for the government in search and rescue. They are very good at their jobs.

Are there certain diseases that golden retrievers are more prone to?

Fortunately, the golden retriever is not prone to any serious diseases. However, they are prone to snow nose. Snow nose is a condition where pink spots emerge on their nose during winter time. These spots tend to disappear during the winter time.

What color are golden retriever dogs?

A golden retriever can come in any color. The color usually ranges from cream to orange. Only after a golden retriever has turned 1 can you truly determine their color.

Do golden retrievers run at a fast pace?

The answer is yes, these dogs run at a very fast pace. They have been known to run for up to 20 to 30 miles per house.

What type of coats do golden retrievers have?

These magnificent dogs have a double coat. Their coats are waterproof and they do a fantastic job of protecting them from both hot and cold.

Is the golden retriever breed famous in Hollywood?

It may not come as a surprise to you but the golden retriever breed has always been famous in Hollywood since the breed was established. In the '80s and 90's they were particularly famous. They starred in many shows and sitcoms such as Empty Nest and Full House.

Has a golden retriever been spotted in The White House?

There was once a very famous golden retriever in The White House. She was beautiful and her name was Liberty. She belonged to the president Gerald Ford. Liberty even had puppies while being in The White House.

Are there any celebrities who own a golden retriever?

There have been many celebrities who have owned a golden retriever dog. Oprah Winfrey, Jimmy Fallon, and Emma Stone are some of the many celebrities who have owned a golden retriever.

Have there been any interesting stories in the news about golden retrievers?

There was a news story about golden retrievers. There was an interesting story where a baby kangaroo thought her mother was a golden retriever. This made news headlines all over Australia.

Have any Guinness World Records been won by a golden retriever?

Believe it or not, a golden retriever dog won the Guinness World Record. This record was won for having the loudest bark of all time. A golden retriever had the loudest bark in the world.

Have there been any accounts of a golden retriever winning a world record?

A remarkable golden retriever won a world record. The world record was won for having the most amount of tennis balls in his mouth. He managed to have five tennis balls in his mouse at the same time. This won the world record.

What was the original purpose of the golden retrievers?

The original reason why golden retrievers were bred was for hunting purposes.

How long has the golden retriever dog been a recognized breed?

The kennel club recognized the very first golden retriever. This took place many years ago back in 1925.

Who bred the very first golden retriever?

The very first golden retriever was bred by a man named Dudley Coutts Marjoribanks. He is responsible for breeding the very first golden retriever.

Which breed of dogs make up the golden retriever?

This dog breed is made up of two breeds. The golden retriever consists of the flat-coated spaniel and the Tweed water spaniel.

Where did the golden retriever breed originate from?

This wonderful breed of dog originated from Scotland many years ago. This was more or less around the 19th century.

CPSIA information can be obtained
at www.ICGtesting.com
Printed in the USA
BVHW021203061220
595044BV00018B/67